Sacramento
CALIFORNIA

Sacramento
CALIFORNIA

DILLON PRESS
Parsippany, New Jersey

by *Terry Janson Dunnahoo*

To my granddaughter Maura
with love

Photo Credits

Front & back cover: Tom Myers Photography.
The Bancroft Library, University of California: 11. Denver Public Library,
Western History Department/Photograph by L.C. McClure: 31. John Elk III:
25. The Granger Collection, New York: 18, 22, 24. Tom Myers Photography:
title page, 27, 49, 54, 57. The Andrew J. Russel Collection, The Oakland
Museum of California: 44. Photo 20–20/Robert Holmes: 9. James Prigoff
Photography: 52. Silver Burdett Ginn: 21. Stock Montage: 41.
Westlight/Craig Aurness: 55; J. Cochrane: 45. Maps, Ortelius Design: 6, 48.

Library of Congress Cataloging-in-Publication Data

Dunnahoo, Terry.
    Sacramento, California/by Terry Janson Dunnahoo. —1st ed.
     p.   cm.—(Places in American history)
    Includes index.
    ISBN 0–382–39333–3 (LSB).—ISBN 0–382–39334–1 (pbk.)
      1. Old Sacramento Historic District (Sacramento, Calif.)—Guidebooks—
Juvenile literature. 2. Sacramento (Calif.)—Guidebooks—Juvenile
literature. 3. Sacramento (Calif.)—History—Juvenile literature. [1. Old
Sacramento Historic District (Sacramento, Calif.). 2. Sacramento (Calif.)—
History.] I. Title. II. Series.
F869.S12D86 1997
917.94'53—dc20
                                        96–11172

Summary: A visit to Old Sacramento, a historical district in California's capital, with restored gold-rush-era buildings, wooden sidewalks, hitching posts,
and cobblestone streets, which bring the city's history to life.

Cover and book design by Lisa Ann Arcuri

 Published by Dillon Press
A Division of Simon & Schuster
299 Jefferson Road, Parsippany, NJ 07054

First Edition

Printed in the United States of America

10 9 8 7 6 5 4 3 2 1

Contents

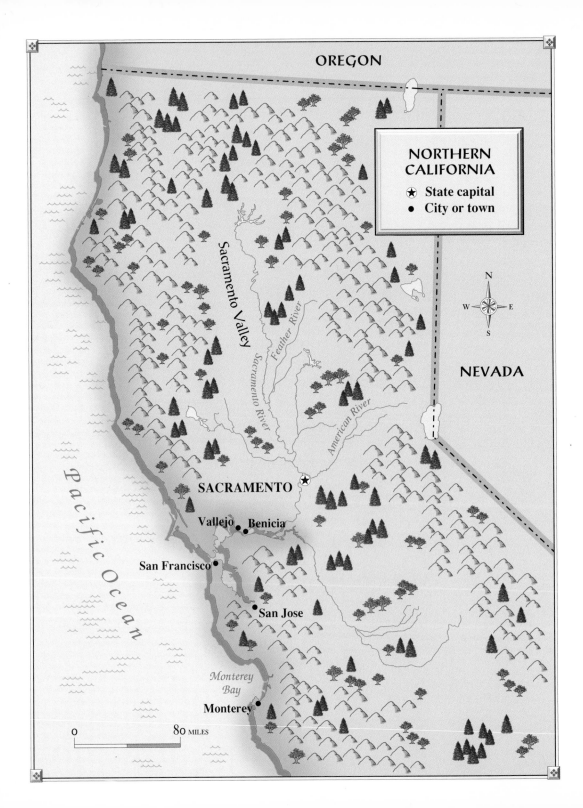

OREGON

NEVADA

NORTHERN
CALIFORNIA

★ State capital
● City or town

Sacramento Valley

Sacramento River

Feather River

American River

Pacific Ocean

SACRAMENTO

Vallejo ● Benicia

San Francisco ●

San Jose ●

Monterey
Bay

Monterey ●

0   80 MILES

CHAPTER 1

A Fort for Protection

Tens of thousands of years ago the ice that covered large areas of North America began to melt. As it melted, rivers and mountains formed. One of these was the Sierra Nevada range. From these mountains came gold that brought thousands of people to California in the 1800s. Many of them helped Sacramento become the capital of California.

But long before Sacramento was the capital of California, Native Americans lived there. Some had wandered to California from Mexico. Some came from the deserts of the United States. Some had walked over a bridge of ice that connected Asia with what is now Alaska.

The Native Americans did not think about gold. They thought about food and spent most of their days looking for it. As long as there was food, Native Americans stayed where they were. When there was no food, they moved to another place.

They ate grasshoppers, lizards, snakes, and worms. They dug for roots, gathered seeds, and picked berries. They made baskets and nets to catch fish. And they killed their prey with spears, clubs, and bows and arrows. To catch a large animal, some Native Americans chased it with relay teams. When one team tired, a new team took over. The runners pursued the animal until it was so tired it fell to the ground. More than 100,000 Native Americans in California lived in this way before explorers came from Spain.

The explorers included Hernán Cortes, who conquered Mexico for Spain, and Juan Rodríguez Cabrillo, who sailed to Monterey Harbor in 1542. These explorers changed the lives of many California Native Americans. But the people who changed their lives the most were the priests from Spain.

The Spaniards built many missions like this one in California.

In 1769, King Charles III of Spain sent soldiers and priests to build churches in California. Captain Gaspar de Portolá was the commanding officer of the soldiers. They built forts and protected the missions, as the churches and surrounding buildings came to be called. Father Junípero Serra was in charge of the missions. He and his priests baptized the Native Americans and made them Christians.

Many Native Americans came to live at the missions. They pounded clay dirt with their hands and feet and added water and straw to make adobe bricks. They used the bricks to build the missions and also to build storehouses, workshops, and tanneries. Workers put the bricks one on top of the other and stuck them together with mud. They made clothes, and they planted seeds to grow food for everybody who lived at the missions.

Now the Native Americans had shelter and a reliable food supply, but they did not have freedom. The priests were always telling them what to do. The priests said that Native Americans who had become Christians had to live at the missions. When the Native Americans ran away, the soldiers brought them back. Sometimes they were whipped.

The priests also said that some day they would give the land and the mission buildings to the Native Americans. Before that day came, however, Mexico declared its independence from Spain. The year was 1821, and the new country was called the Mexican Republic. All Spanish-born priests

In this painting, Native Americans of California are shown at a Spanish mission.

were ordered to leave California. The Mexican Republic took the mission lands and the buildings, and the Native Americans never received what the priests had promised.

Although the Spaniards had established many missions in California, there was never a mission in Sacramento. In 1808, Gabriel Moraga explored the Central Valley of California. He told the priests that there was no good place for a mission in the valley. He named the area *Sacramento,* the Spanish word for "sacrament." Sacramento still does not have a mission, but it does have Sutter's Fort. This fort was the beginning of the city of Sacramento.

The man who built the fort was Johann August Suter. In 1834 he sailed from Europe to the United States. He told his wife and five children he would send for them when he was settled. They begged him to stay. But he owed money to many people. If he had not left, he would have gone to jail.

Suter changed his name to John Augustus Sutter and settled in Missouri. As a trader, he traveled to Santa Fe, in New Mexico; the Rocky Mountains; and Fort Vancouver, in the Oregon Territory. During his travels, Sutter learned that the Mexican government was giving away land to settlers. A group of trappers told him about the Sacramento Valley. Plants and fruit grew wild there, and the rivers were filled with fish. Sutter decided to settle there.

In 1838 he waited in Fort Vancouver for a ship to take him from the Columbia River to Monterey. But each day he was told there was no room for him. Tired of waiting, Sutter boarded a ship bound for the Sandwich Islands, now the state of Hawaii.

From there he planned to take a ship to
California. Months later he was still waiting.

Finally, Sutter hired a ship, filled it with
cargo, and sailed to Sitka, Alaska. With him were
ten Hawaiians who had agreed to work for him.
He also took three cannons to defend the land he
planned to own. In Sitka, Sutter sold and traded
his cargo. Then he sailed for Monterey, where the
Mexican Republic had government offices.

On the way, storms almost tore the ship
apart. Sutter entered the harbor at Yerba Buena,
now San Francisco, to make repairs. Mariano
Vallejo, the military commander, told Sutter that
the only port that accepted ships from foreign
countries was Monterey. Sutter had come from
Alaska, which then belonged to Russia. Sutter
would not give up. He talked Vallejo into letting
him repair the ship. Two days later, Sutter sailed
to Monterey.

On July 5, 1839, he met with the Mexican
governor in the area, Juan Bautista Alvarado,
who had fought for independence from Spain.

Sutter asked for permission to build a settlement in the Sacramento Valley. Sutter said he would build houses, grow crops, and raise cattle. He would build a blacksmith shop, a carpenter shop, and a candle shop. He would build whatever the settlement needed. And he would build a fort to protect everything.

Governor Alvarado liked what he heard. Maybe Sutter could keep squatters away. Maybe he could scare off trappers. Maybe he could do something about the Native Americans. They had raided Mexican camps and stolen horses. Worse, they had stolen guns. Governor Alvarado was worried.

He was also worried about losing land owned by the Mexican Republic to other countries. Two years earlier a United States ship had sailed the Sacramento River. A British ship had also sailed the river. And Russia's Fort Ross was not far away. The governor believed that if there were a settlement in the Sacramento Valley, foreign governments might stay away from land owned by the Mexican Republic.

Governor Alvarado told Sutter to explore the river until he found the land he wanted to settle. If Sutter kept his promises for a year, Governor Alvarado would make him a Mexican citizen. And Sutter would own the land he settled. Sutter thanked the governor and went to San Francisco to buy boats, tools, and farming equipment. At Fort Ross he bought cattle and horses that would be taken up the river later.

After eight days Sutter and his workers reached the place where the Sacramento and the American rivers meet. He thought of settling there but decided to keep going. A bit farther Sutter stopped. He liked this land. It would yield food for the settlement. Clumps of trees dotted the area. They would shade the cattle, and there was a hill that was perfect for a fort.

Sutter had his workers carry to shore the cannons he had brought from the Sandwich Islands. Then they pitched tents. Later Sutter wrote that the date was August 12, 1839. He added that he had a bulldog and 18 workers, including the 10 Hawaiians. The Hawaiians built houses with grass the way they did in the Sandwich Islands.

By the summer of 1840, there was a house built with bricks made of straw and mud. Wheat, barley, beans, and cotton had been planted. Mules pulled plows in the fields. Cattle and sheep grazed. Adobe bricks for more buildings were drying in the sun. And Sutter's workers had cleared a two-mile path from the fort to the river so that he could send and receive goods.

Eventually, Native Americans also worked with Sutter. When he first came to the valley, they robbed him, killed cattle, and stole horses. The bulldog and the cannons scared the Native Americans away. Sutter wrote in his diary that the dog had saved his life three times. And he wrote that the Native Americans signed a peace treaty after 30 were killed while attacking the fort. Sutter also wrote later that Native Americans became his best friends.

CHAPTER 2

War and Gold

On August 29, 1841, Sutter went to Monterey. Governor Alvarado made him a citizen of the Mexican Republic and gave Sutter the land that Sutter had worked on all year. Governor Alvarado also made him a representative of the Mexican Republic. This gave Sutter power over everyone on his land. He returned to the fort with more workers. One was a barrel maker, who was the first African American to live in the Sacramento Valley.

Sutter wore military clothes and called himself Captain Sutter. Others called him Captain, too. He named his settlement New Helvetia. *Helvetia* is the Latin word for "Switzerland." His parents were German and

Portrait of John Sutter in his captain uniform

Swiss, and Sutter wanted to honor Switzerland. So he flew the faded Swiss flag he had brought from Europe. And, as a citizen of the Mexican Republic, he flew the Mexican flag.

Sutter liked being important, and he liked owning land. He built a cattle ranch on the Feather River and called it Hock Farm. In September, Sutter bought Fort Ross from Russia. He agreed to pay $30,000 for the fort and gave the Russians $2,000. He promised to pay the rest of the debt with crops and money. From Fort Ross, Sutter moved a boat; 2,000 horses, mules and sheep; and other goods to his fort. About 100 of the animals died. Sutter used the hides to make leather.

He built guest houses outside the fort. More and more people came. Some rested for a time and moved on. Others settled near the fort. All of Sutter's dreams were coming true.

In November 1845, General José Castro came from Monterey to Sutter's Fort. There was talk of war with the United States. If attacked, the thick walls of the fort could protect the surrounding land. Castro offered Sutter $100,000 for the fort.

With that much money, Sutter could pay what he owed to the Russians. And he could bring his wife and children from Europe. Sutter went to his office to talk with friends. They talked a long time. If he sold the fort, what would happen to the settlers in the Sacramento Valley? Who would protect them? Who would help settlers already on their way to California? Sutter told General Castro the fort was not for sale.

By May 1846 the United States and the Mexican Republic were at war. Many American settlers had been unhappy with the way the Mexican government had treated them. In the middle of June, some settlers surrounded the home of Mariano Vallejo, in Sonoma. He represented the Mexican Republic and had a few soldiers. But there were not enough to defeat the settlers. The settlers declared Sonoma free from the Mexican Republic.

The settlers needed a flag, so they painted a bear and a star on white cloth. At the bottom they put a red stripe and wrote the words *California Republic*. They called their rebellion the Bear Flag Revolt.

William B. Ide, a schoolteacher, was elected commander of the group. The rebels brought their Mexican prisoners to the fort and told Sutter to put Vallejo and the others in his prison. Sutter would not do it. Ide insisted, but Sutter

The Bear Flag

said no. Ide lost the argument. But he gave orders that the Mexican flag be taken down and the Bear Flag raised instead.

The Bear Flag did not stay on the fort's flagpole long. Joseph Warren Revere, a descendent of Paul Revere who fought in the Revolutionary War, replaced the Bear Flag with a United States flag. Within a few days, Sutter's Fort had flown the flag of the Mexican Republic, the Bear Flag, and the United States flag. Sutter wondered if the United States government would keep his property forever.

Shortly after the Bear Flag Revolt, United States Captain John Drake Sloat sailed his ship into Monterey Harbor. The Mexican flag was

In this drawing the United States flag flies above Sutter's Fort.

lowered, and the United States flag was raised on Colton Hall. The flag was also raised in San Jose, Sonoma, San Francisco, and other cities. This happened so quickly that Mexican Republic citizens in these areas surrendered. Fighting continued in the southern part of the California Territory until January 13, 1847.

In March the United States government gave Sutter all his property back. He hired more workers. People came to buy food, clothes, blankets, saddles, spurs, and other articles the workers made. Sutter's cattle were healthy. Various grains, fruits, and vegetables grew in the fields. He had all these things, but he needed lumber.

In August, Sutter asked James Wilson Marshall, one of his carpenters, to search for a place that had streams swift enough to run a sawmill. In return for the work, Sutter would give Marshall a share of the lumber. Marshall found a place the Native Americans called Colloomah, which means "beautiful valley." It was on the American River in the foothills of the Sierra Nevada, about 50 miles from Sutter's Fort. Sutter leased the land from the Native Americans.

Marshall hired workers to build Sutter's Mill. They dug a ditch and built a dam. Every night, Marshall let the stream run through the ditch to wash out dirt and gravel. On January 24, 1848, he saw something glitter in the dirt and gravel. He picked up a piece of yellow metal. Gold! Could it be gold?

Marshall rolled a nugget in his fingers. If this was fool's gold, the nugget would break into bits.

An etching of Sutter's Mill on the American River, where gold was discovered in 1848

He pounded it with a rock. The metal flattened but did not break. Marshall wrapped the nugget in a rag and jumped on his horse. Rain had washed away some of the trails Marshall and his workers had cleared in August, and he had to clear new ones. It took four days to get to the fort. Marshall raced into Sutter's office, dripping rainwater all over the floor. Sutter stared at the nugget in the rag. Then he grabbed a book and began to read about metals. When he finished reading, he knew that Marshall had found real gold.

Sutter could not leave the fort right away. He told Marshall to go back to the sawmill and protect the gold. A few days later, when Sutter reached the sawmill, workers had gold in their pockets. Some had gold in their hats. One man was limping. He had gold in his shoes. Sutter told the workers they had to give him the gold. They did, but he wondered if they gave all they had.

Sutter and Marshall found gold in every stream, creek, and ravine near Sutter's Mill. If his workers left him to dig for gold, Sutter would have nobody to work at the fort and the settlement. He promised the millworkers they could keep all the gold they found on Sundays, their day off. If they kept the secret from workers at the fort, Sutter promised to double their wages.

The millworkers agreed, but the secret leaked out. On March 7, Sutter wrote in his journal that everybody, including his clerk and his cook, had left him. This may be an exaggeration. But so many workers left that most of Sutter's crops rotted in the fields.

CHAPTER 3

A City Grows

Samuel Brannan, a friend of Sutter's, had come to San Francisco from New York in July 1846 and worked as a laborer. The next year, Brannan started the first newspaper in San Francisco. When Brannan heard rumors about gold, he went to the gold fields and streams to see if the rumors were true.

At the gold fields, Brannan saw so much gold that he wondered why more people in San Francisco were not searching for the precious metal. He learned that his editor had written articles stating that rumors about finding gold were false. To prove that the rumors were true, Brannan put gold dust and a tiny nugget in a bottle and went to San Francisco. He let people

Gold nuggets like the ones prospectors would have found during the gold rush

run gold through their fingers. The feel of gold sent people to the gold fields. So many rushed there that fewer than 100 people were left in San Francisco.

Brannan had built a store on Sutter's property near the fort. Now he loaded the store with blankets, tents, picks, shovels, and pans that miners who came from the East would need to look for gold. Then he built a second store along the river about two miles from the fort. The river was where people who came from other areas would stop to get supplies before going to the gold fields.

Sutter wrote in his journal that people came to look for gold from "South America, Mexico, the Sandwich Islands, etc." Some crossed the Pacific. Some crossed the Atlantic. Some sailed around South America's Cape Horn. Others came overland in wagon trains, and some even walked. Many of these people stopped at the fort. They were called forty-niners, for 1849—the year many gold-seekers went to California.

Sutter tried to run his settlement the way he always had. He fed people and let them borrow horses to get to the gold fields. The horses were not returned. Rustlers killed his cattle and sold the meat at mining camps. Some settlers bought land from him, but most just stole the land.

Sutter was still in debt to the Russians for Fort Ross. They threatened to take what was left of his settlement. To try to get money, Sutter took a crew of Native Americans and some Hawaiians to mine for gold. The crew learned quickly that gold mining was hard work. They went back to the fort. Sutter wrote to his son John Augustus,

Jr., in Europe and asked him to come to the fort. When he arrived in September, Sutter gave his son the property. Because of this action, the Russians could not take the land.

While Sutter was losing much of his property, Brannan was building a two-story hotel. By the end of May, there were 30 buildings along the river. Boats became warehouses and were called store ships. Boats were also used as stores. Even the post office and the jail were on boats. The area was called the Embarcadero, the Spanish word for "landing." Sutter's son liked the way the Embarcadero was growing, but Sutter did not like it. This was not the port he had imagined.

To feed the newcomers, more and more eating places sprang up. Most were made of wood and boat sails, and signs invited people to eat. "Come in the inn and take a bite" said one sign. "Eating is done here" said another.

Boats arrived at the Embarcadero both day and night. Wagons and carts were loaded and unloaded. Garbage was dumped everywhere.

Carts sprinkled water on the dirt streets to keep the dust down. Everybody fought mosquitoes, fleas, and bedbugs. People itched and scratched, itched and scratched. Noise from mule trains leaving for the gold fields, barking dogs, and crying children kept nearly everybody awake at night.

At the gold fields, people claimed land and mined for gold. Most prospectors were honest and hardworking. They worked hours and hours every day to find the gold they dug from the hillsides or panned from the rivers. Sometimes thieves stole their gold. Often there were fights and murders. With no laws, there was frontier justice. Miners decided who lived or died.

Miners also decided where Asians, African Americans, and Mexicans could search for gold. These groups were sent away from one mine after another and had to go higher and higher into the hills to dig. Mexicans complained that a few years earlier, this had been their land. But now if they wanted to look for gold, they had to go high into the hills.

A prospector panning for gold

With hundreds of people landing at the Embarcadero every day, laws were needed. Legislators in the United States Congress had talked and talked about what to do with the land won from the Mexican Republic. Congress was still talking. So some residents met under an oak tree near the Sacramento River and took action. They drew boundaries and called the area Sacramento City. Sutter's son voted for the name. Sutter argued that the city should be called Sutterville.

From September to November 1849, 48 delegates from California met at Colton Hall in Monterey. One of them was Sutter. Some of the delegates had fought against the United States. But now they joined their former enemies to write a state constitution and to demand that California be admitted to the Union.

The delegates set up elections and ordered that children be educated. They wrote a plan that would allow women to keep the property they owned before they were married. And they voted to make San Jose the capital of the new state.

Colton Hall in Monterey, California

When Sacramento City residents asked why their city was not chosen to be the capital, the delegates said it was because of the gold. When the gold was gone from the mountains, they said, Sacramento City would become a ghost town. But San Jose was an old city that would always be there. It was settled in 1777, one year after the Declaration of Independence was signed.

Delegates met in San Jose in December. They learned that the city was not only old, it was hard to reach. They complained that there were not enough comfortable places to eat and sleep. Mariano Vallejo, one of the delegates, promised to build a capital city at Vallejo, the city to which he gave his name. The other delegates accepted his offer.

In January 1850, after weeks of heavy rains, the Sacramento and American rivers rushed over their banks and flooded Sacramento City. Goods on the Embarcadero floated away. Buildings toppled like houses of cards, and tents were swept away. One man jumped into a boat, which sank. The gold in the belly belt tied around his waist was so heavy that he could not swim. Bystanders called out to him to untie the belt, but he would not listen. He drowned with the gold still tied around his waist.

The rain finally stopped. By January 18 most of the city had been dug out, and people started building again. They constructed ditches, channels, and dams, which they should have done earlier. Over the years, Native Americans talked about "great waters" that had covered the valley 45 years earlier. In the years since, there had been other "great waters." Sutter had heard about these floods from Native Americans. This was why he had chosen high ground for his settlement.

CHAPTER 4

School, Pony Express, and Trains

On September 9, 1850, President Millard Fillmore signed the document that made California the thirty-first state. People in Sacramento City did not learn about the event until the middle of October. At two o'clock in the morning, the river steamer *New World* anchored in Sacramento City, bringing news of California's admission to the Union. People cheered and danced. Some raced their horses through the city, shouting the news.

The California Statehood Charter papers were brought from the East Coast by 17-year-old Mary Helen Crosby. She was the daughter of a New York lawyer and was on her way to visit an aunt in Sacramento City. Mary Helen had been asked to put the papers in a safe place, and she hid them in her clothes and under her pillow. When she crossed the Isthmus of Panama, she hid the papers in her closed umbrella. People there often stole from travelers crossing the isthmus.

When California became a state, Sutter became a citizen of the United States. He brought his wife, Annette, and his other children from Europe. He took his land back from his son to try to save what was left of his property. But Sutter could not save much of the land he had worked so hard to own. The fort had been sold, and squatters had taken most of his land in the Sacramento Valley. Sutter went to live at Hock Farm with his family.

When the state legislators met in San Jose in 1851, they voted to drop the word *city* from Sacramento City. Most citizens thought that Sacramento was a better name. Sutter still wished the city had been called Sutterville.

When the legislators finished their business in San Jose, they hoped that the new capital at

Vallejo would be ready for their next meeting. In 1852, Vallejo was still not ready. Sacramento offered its courthouse, and the delegates agreed to meet there. Sacramento served as the capital while the legislators were there, but San Jose was still the permanent capital.

In April the governor of California ordered that all state records be sent from San Jose to the city of Vallejo. This was a sign that Vallejo would become the permanent capital. But in 1853, Vallejo was still not ready for the legislators. Angry at the delays, they conducted legislative business in Benicia.

Sacramento would have invited the legislators to meet in their courthouse again. But in November 1852 more than half of Sacramento had burned. The fire started in a hat shop. With bucket brigades and water from the Sacramento River, citizens worked tirelessly to put out the fires. Even so, by dawn hundreds of houses, stores, churches, and government buildings had burned to ashes.

In 1854 and 1855 the legislators met in Sacramento again. Sacramento citizens had offered to build a capitol building for the legislature, and Sacramento now became the permanent capital of California. No state in the country has had as many capitals as California.

When the legislators had met in Monterey in 1849, they agreed that children should be educated. A few private schools had opened. But it wasn't until February 20, 1854, that a public school opened, at 5th and K streets, in Sacramento. It did not open sooner because of fires, floods, and construction delays. In addition, the school committee could not agree on how to run the schools.

On the first day of school, 50 boys and 40 girls attended. The boys had a male teacher. The girls had a female teacher. Four days later there were 90 boys and 70 girls. Because the school was overcrowded, a second building was opened. A year later there was not enough money to keep the schools open, so the Lee and Marshall Circus gave a benefit show to raise money.

After school, children rolled barrel hoops on the dirt streets to amuse themselves. They spun tops made from acorns. They carved whistles out of wood and made fiddles, kites, and puppets. And they swam in the Sacramento River.

Now that children were going to school, the city needed a library. In October 1857, citizens organized the Sacramento Library Association. A building at 5th and J streets became the first public library. People gave money and books. And the city of New York sent 800 books. It took a long time for the books to reach Sacramento. Everything took a long time to reach Sacramento.

Stagecoaches had been traveling between Missouri and California since the late 1850s. These coaches covered the hundreds of miles in about three weeks, bringing passengers, packages, and mail to Sacramento. But people wanted their mail even faster. In 1860 the Pony Express began, and they got their wish.

The Pony Express owners built 190 stations, bought 500 horses, and hired 80 riders who were

A Pony Express rider en route to California

all about 18 years old. Riders had to be strong and light. The thinner the riders were, the better. Armed with only a knife and a revolver, they carried the mail.

Pony Express riders rode alone through blizzards and thunderstorms and faced other dangers such as mountain lions and packs of wolves. They galloped day and night in relays of 75 to 100 miles. They had two minutes to stretch and change horses. Two of the riders were William Frederick "Buffalo Bill" Cody and James Butler "Wild Bill" Hickok.

The first Pony Express run left St. Joseph, Missouri, on April 3, 1860, and reached Sacramento on April 13. Residents closed their stores, sang, danced, and shot cannons that scared the Pony Express rider and his horse. The end of the ride was at the B.F. Hastings Building. The Pony Express lasted just 18 months. Telegraph companies put it out of business after completion of a transcontinental telegraph line in 1861, linking East to West. Now people could send messages across telegraph wires from the Pacific to the Atlantic.

Soon some people used the new telegraph wires to tell others that Sacramento was flooded again. In December 1861 and January 1862, the Sacramento and American rivers raged over their banks. Newspaper headlines reported that this was the worst flood ever. Newspaper editorials also said that Sacramento should not be the capital. It was foolish to have a capital located in a city that flooded every few years.

Because of the flood, the legislators held their sessions in San Francisco. There was talk that

San Francisco should become the permanent capital. Other citizens asked that their city become the state capital. But the people of Sacramento had worked hard to make their city the capital. They were determined not to give up this honor.

By summer, workers had started raising the city to keep flood waters out. Government buildings, houses, and stores were lifted with giant jackscrews. Sometimes one building was raised, but the one beside it was not. Ramps and stairs were built so that people could go from one level to another without injury. People called Sacramento the city on stilts. By 1873 the project was completed. Dirt dredged from the American River had been used to raise most of downtown Sacramento by 12 feet.

The first train track of the Sacramento Valley Railroad had been laid on August 9, 1855. It connected Sacramento with mining towns along the 22 miles of tracks. For years the United States Congress had talked about a transcontinental railroad, but nothing came of it until President

Workers and officials gathered at Promontory Point in Utah for a ceremony to mark the completion of the transcontinental railroad.

Abraham Lincoln signed the Pacific Railroad Bill in July 1862. The Civil War had started in April 1861, and the country needed railroads to move people and supplies. In Sacramento, work on the western portion of the transcontinental railroad began in January 1863.

Thousands of laborers from different ethnic groups built the railroad. Many Asians left the gold fields to work on the railroads. They made up almost 90 percent of the laborers on the Central Pacific Railroad. Everyone worked 12 hours a day, 6 days a week. While these people worked from west to east, others worked from

The California State Capitol

east to west. When the workers and the tracks met on May 10, 1869, a telegraph message flashed across the country from Promontory Point, Utah. "The last spike driven. Pacific Railroad is completed!" The United States now had a railroad that connected the Pacific coast to the Atlantic coast.

The California State Capitol was also completed in 1869. John Augustus Sutter was not in Sacramento when the railroad and the capitol were completed. In 1865, after fire destroyed the barn and other buildings at Hock Farm, he and his wife moved to Washington, D.C. For 15 years, Sutter asked Congress to give him money for the property that the gold seekers had stolen from him. He died on June 18, 1880, having received no property or money. Sutter had never returned to Sacramento, the city he wanted to name Sutterville.

CHAPTER 5

A Walk Through the Past

Finding the locations of historical places in Sacramento is easy. Builders of the city in the 1840s used numbers and letters of the alphabet to name the streets.

Sutter's Fort State Historic Park is bordered by K and L streets and by 26th and 28th streets. When you walk through the gates of the fort, you step back in time to 1846. Dressed in pioneer costumes, volunteers answer questions and give demonstrations of how people lived at the fort. Sutter's bedroom is to the left. The room has a small bed, a candle, a wash bowl, a pitcher, and a chamber pot.

Between the candle shop and the coal bin is the blacksmith shop. Tools, plows, axes, shovels, wheels,

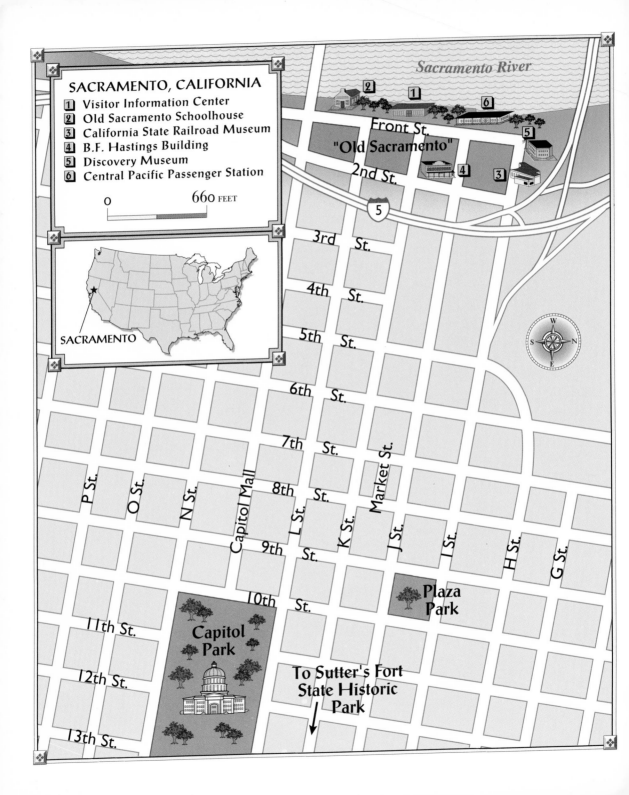

SACRAMENTO, CALIFORNIA

1 Visitor Information Center
2 Old Sacramento Schoolhouse
3 California State Railroad Museum
4 B.F. Hastings Building
5 Discovery Museum
6 Central Pacific Passenger Station

0   660 FEET

SACRAMENTO

Sacramento River

Front St.

"Old Sacramento"

2nd St.

5

3rd St.

4th St.

5th St.

6th St.

7th St.

P St.

O St.

N St.

Capitol Mall

8th St.

L St.

K St.

Market St.

J St.

I St.

H St.

G St.

9th St.

Plaza Park

10th St.

11th St.

Capitol Park

12th St.

To Sutter's Fort State Historic Park

13th St.

At Sutter's Fort State Park, volunteers dressed in pioneer costumes demonstrate how people lived at the fort.

and animal traps were made there. Now volunteers show visitors how these things were made.

At the gristmill, oxen walked around and around a pole to crush grains that workers had planted and harvested. The Native Americans separated the kernels from dirt and rocks. The kernels were washed and then ground into flour to make bread and other food. The oxen are gone now, but visitors are invited to help crush grains with stones.

Wooden barrels, tubs, and pails are made in the cooper's shop. There is a bakery, a weaving room, a saddle room, and a carpenter shop. Sutter's headquarters were in the large building that is located in the center of the fort.

A bedroom at Sutter's Fort State Historic Park

In October, tour guides dress like hunters, traders, and trappers to reenact a hunting trip along the banks of the Sacramento River. During the month-long trip from Red Bluff to Sacramento, they set up camps. There they interpret the life and times of the traders and trappers who came to the Sacramento Valley during the 1830s and 1840s.

The California State Capitol is bound by L and N streets and 10th and 15th streets. There are museum rooms, and you can see a film that explains the history of the capitol. Volunteers will take you on a tour. You can sit in the galleries to watch how California legislators pass laws. You may even see them vote on proposed laws.

The capitol is surrounded by Capitol Park. The park is filled with trees from all over the world. When children go on field trips to the capitol, they sit on the grass while they eat their lunches. They can feed the squirrels. They walk on a map that shows the missions that Father Serra and the Native Americans built. There is a statue of Father Serra. His big toe is shiny because many children rub it for luck before they go back to class.

Old Sacramento is a National Landmark, and part of the area is a California state park. Old Sacramento is bordered by the Sacramento River, 2nd Street, and M and I streets. Old Sacramento was the center of the city in the 1800s. Over the years businesses moved away and the area became a slum. In the 1960s it was rebuilt.

The Visitor Information Center is on Front Street at the end of K Street. You may get maps there. Then walk down the wooden sidewalks.

A statue of Father Junipero Serra stands in Capitol Park.

You may see the Living History Program Players dressed in old-fashioned clothes. Ask questions. They can tell you about the floods and the fires. They can tell you how the Central Pacific Railroad was built. You may bump into a Pony Express rider. Maybe he will tell you how tired he was after his hundred-mile ride.

You can also take a ride in a carriage pulled by horses with names like Molly, Anne, and Roany. Drivers are dressed like old-timers with checkered shirts, weather-beaten hats, and dusty boots. The carriages and wagons look like the ones on the streets of Sacramento in the 1800s. Listen to the clippity-clop rhythm of the horses' hooves on cobblestones.

There are several museums in Old Sacramento. One is a reconstructed one-room schoolhouse on Front Street, at the end of L Street. The school has desks, books, lessons, and a chalkboard used in the 1800s. A round black stove stands in the middle of the room. Outside, a swing hangs from a tree. The wooden seat is tied

Costumed guides stroll the streets in Old Sacramento.

Visitors can walk through old train cars at the California State Railroad Museum.

to a rope with a big knot. The bathroom is a small wooden building in the corner of the schoolyard.

The California State Railroad Museum, one of California's best museums, is at 2nd and I streets. The Sacramento Valley Railroad and the Central Pacific Railroad began in Old Sacramento. The museum has locomotives and train cars. Walk through them to see how people slept on long trips. A sleeping car simulates the swaying motion on the tracks. See how the mail was sorted while the trains raced along. From exhibits, learn why Asians made up 90 percent of the laborers during the building of the Central Pacific Railroad. View the dioramas, murals, and films that tell the story of American railroads.

Across from the Railroad Museum is the Central Pacific Passenger Station. This was the first depot for the transcontinental railroad. Take a self-guided tour with an audio-wand. The tape in the wand will tell you what kinds of trains people rode on, where they ate, and what they wore.

The B.F. Hastings Building at 2nd and J streets was built immediately after the 1852 fire. It opened as a bank. It was also used by the California Supreme Court justices from 1855 to 1859, the year they moved into the capitol. The B.F. Hastings Building served also as the Pony Express terminal, the telegraph office, and the Sacramento office of the Wells Fargo Bank.

A riverboat carries tourists on the Sacramento River.

Now the building is a museum that exhibits a Wells Fargo office of the 1800s. You can see gold dust, gold samples, a scale to measure gold, and tools that miners used. And you can send a telegraph message in code the way Wells Fargo agents did more than a hundred years ago. On the second floor, visit the rooms that the California Supreme Court Justices used during 1855–1859.

The Discovery Museum, at the end of I Street, has exhibits about history and agriculture.

Its science and technology exhibits have a variety of demonstrations including "Electricity Everyday Magic." The museum also has a working historical print shop and a gold collection worth a million dollars.

On the river, where gold seekers came by the thousands, there are riverboat cruises. Watch the Tower Bridge rise when tall boats pass through. Keep an eye out for beavers, otters, and blue herons. And imagine that you are a forty-niner landing on shore, eager to get to the gold fields to search for gold.

Sacramento, California:
A HISTORICAL TIME LINE

1542   Juan Rodríguez Cabrillo sails into Monterey Bay.

1808   Gabriel Moraga explores the Sacramento Valley.

1821   Mexico declares its independence from Spain.

1834   Johann Augustus Sutter sails from Europe to the United States.

1839   Sutter settles in the Sacramento Valley.

1841   Sutter becomes a citizen of the Mexican Republic.

1846   The United States and Mexico are at war. Bear Flag Revolt
Sutter loses his property to the United States government.
John Drake Sloat takes control of Monterey.

1847   Sutter becomes a United States citizen and his land is returned to him.

1848   James Marshall finds gold.

1849   Sutter gives land to his son to save it from squatters and debt collectors.
First California State Constitutional Convention is held in Monterey.

1850 California becomes the thirty-first state in the Union.

Sutter's wife and his other children come to Sacramento City.

Flooding from the Sacramento River and American River covers most of the city.

1852 Most of Sacramento burns when fire breaks out.

1854 Fire destroys most of the city again.

Sacramento becomes the capital of California.

The first public school opens.

1857 The first library opens.

1860 The Pony Express begins delivering mail.

1863 Central Pacific Railroad workers begin laying tracks for the transcontinental railroad.

1865 Sutter moves to Washington, D.C., with his wife.

1869 Central Pacific Railroad and Union Pacific Railroad tracks meet at Promontory Point, Utah.

California State Capitol is completed.

1880 Sutter dies in Washington, D.C., without recovering his property.

Visitor Information

Sutter's Fort State Historic Park—bordered by K and L streets and by 26th and 28th streets. Guided tours. Also self-guided tours with audio-wands that explain the exhibit rooms. Open daily 10:00 A.M. to 5:00 P.M. Admission: $2.00 for adults, $1.00 for children under 18. Living History Program on Tuesdays and Thursdays from November to June: $5.00 for adults, $2.00 for children.

California State Capitol—bordered by L and N streets and 10th and 15th streets. Guided public tours daily on the hour. Open from 9:00 A.M. to 5:00 P.M. Admission: free

Old Sacramento—a National Landmark. Part of the area is a California state park. It is bound by M and I streets and Front and 2nd streets.

The following places are all in Old Sacramento.

Old Sacramento Schoolhouse—Front Street at the end of L Street. Reconstructed one-room school-house, open Monday through Friday 9:30 A.M. to 4:00 P.M., Saturday and Sunday noon to 4:00 P.M., volunteer staff permitting. Admission: free.

California State Railroad Museum—2nd and I streets. Open daily 10:00 A.M. to 5:00 P.M. Self-guided tour tells the history of California rail-roading. Restored locomotives and train cars, exhibits, hundreds of artifacts, dioramas, and a movie. Admission: $5.00 for adults, $2.00 for children 6 to 12, free for children under 6. Tickets for this museum are valid at the Central Pacific Passenger station on day of purchase.

Central Pacific Passenger Station—Front and J streets. Open daily 10:00 A.M. to 5:00 P.M. Station depicts the bustling activities of train travel in the mid-1800s. Steam-powered train rides available every weekend, April through Labor Day, from 10:00 A.M. to 5:00 P.M.; October through December, on the first weekend of the month from noon to 3:00 P.M. Train fares: $5.00 for adults, $2.00 for children 6 to 12, free for children 5 and under.

B.F. Hastings Building—2nd and J streets. Open Tuesday through Sunday 10:00 A.M. to 5:00 P.M. Gold samples, gold scales, and tools. Reconstructed California State Supreme Court chambers of the 1850s. Admission: free.

Discovery Museum—101 I Street. Summer hours: Tuesday through Sunday 10:00 A.M. to 5:00 P.M. Winter hours: Wednesday through Friday noon to 5:00 P.M. Admission: $3.50 for adults, $2.00 for children 6 to 17, free for children under 6.

Index